OUR ANGRY PLANET

Earthquakes

JEN GREEN

Adapted from an original text by Anne Rooney

W
FRANKLIN WATTS
LONDON • SYDNEY

First published in 2009 by Franklin Watts

Copyright © 2009 Arcturus Publishing Limited

Franklin Watts
338 Euston Road
London NW1 3BH

Franklin Watts Australia
Level 17/207 Kent Street, Sydney, NSW 2000

Produced by Arcturus Publishing Limited,
26/27 Bickels Yard, 151–153 Bermondsey Street, London SE1 3HA

Our Angry Planet is based on the series *Nature's Fury*, published by Franklin Watts.

Editor: Alex Woolf
Designer: Mind's Eye Design and Mike Reynolds

Picture Credits
Corbis: 4 (Bettmann), 15 (Vanni Archive), 17 (Eriko Sugita/Reuters), 18 (Roger Ressmeyer), 19 (Lloyd Cluff), 20 (Patrick Robert/Sygma), 22 (Reuters), 27 (Peter Turnley), 29 (Mimmo Jodice).
Rex Features: 5 (Sipa Press), 9 (Araldo di Crollalanza), 11 (Roy Garner), 13 (Sipa Press), 14 (DigitalGlobe), 21 (Roger-Viollet), 23 (Sipa Press), 24 (Action Press), 26 (Dan Tuffs), 28 (Denis Cameron).
Science Photo Library: 6 (Gary Hincks), 7 (Roger Harris), 8 (Christian Darkin), 10 (Gary Hincks), 12 (Gary Hincks), 16 (Mauro Fermariello), 25 (Peter Menzel).
Shutterstock: cover (robert paul van beets).

Every attempt has been made to clear copyright. Should there be any inadvertent omission, please apply to the publisher for rectification.

A CIP catalogue record for this book is available from the British Library.

Dewey Decimal Classification Number: 551.22

ISBN 978 0 7496 9046 5

Printed in China

Franklin Watts is a division of Hachette Children's Books, an Hachette UK Company
www.hachette.co.uk

Contents

What are Earthquakes?

When an earthquake hits, the ground shakes violently. Roads and bridges twist and shatter. Buildings come crashing to the ground.

Rippling ground

Shock waves from an earthquake spread through the ground like ripples spread through water. People a long way away can feel the shaking. Distant homes can be damaged by the quake.

▼ A massive earthquake wrecked Tokyo in 1650.

Country and city

When an earthquake strikes a built-up area, thousands of people may die. As buildings topple, falling bricks and **debris** can kill or injure people.

Out in the countryside, fewer homes are at risk. However, earthquakes may still kill by triggering other hazards. They can cause **landslides**, **avalanches**, floods and giant waves called **tsunamis**.

Past and present

Ever since the Earth formed, there have been earthquakes. In days gone by, people believed that angry gods sent these terrible disasters.

THE LEGEND OF NAMAZU

Japan is regularly hit by earthquakes. Long ago, people believed that these were caused by a giant catfish called the Namazu. It lived in the mud under Japan. Most of the time, a god pressed it down with a huge stone, so the fish was quiet. But sometimes it escaped and thrashed wildly. This caused an earthquake.

▲ **Thousands died when an earthquake hit Mexico City in 1985.**

Each year, more than 50,000 earthquakes happen somewhere on Earth. However, most of these are tiny – so small that they go unnoticed.

Patchwork of Plates

Earth's surface is not one continuous layer, like the smooth surface of an egg. If it was, earthquakes might not happen. Instead, Earth's surface is made up of many pieces that fit together like a cracked eggshell.

Cracked crust

Earth's hard, rocky surface is called the **crust**. It is made up of huge sections called **tectonic plates**. There are seven enormous plates and more than 20 smaller ones.

Six of the large plates carry both land and sea. The seventh lies below the vast Pacific Ocean. The crust below the land is thicker and older than the crust beneath the ocean.

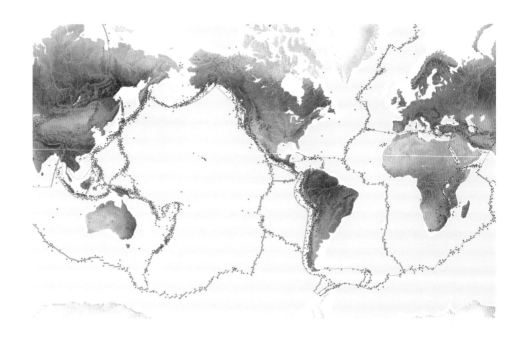

▶ **This map shows Earth's tectonic plates. Most earthquakes strike along plate borders, as shown by the red dots.**

Below the crust

Beneath the crust is a deep layer of hot, semi-liquid rock. This layer is called the **mantle**. The rock here flows very slowly, like hot treacle. Tectonic plates float on top like crusts on a simmering soup.

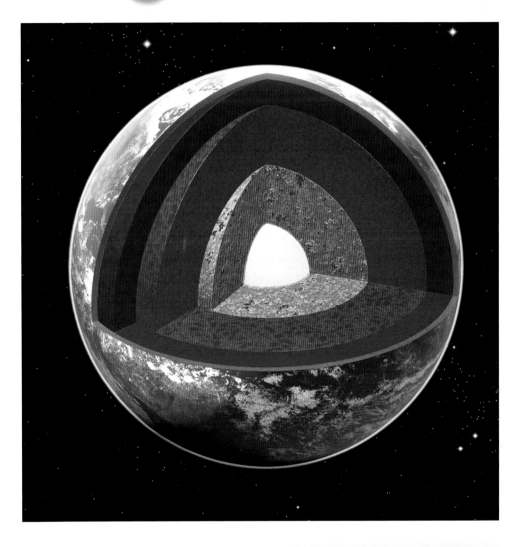

▲ This diagram shows the inner structure of the Earth.

INSIDE THE EARTH

Earth's crust is fairly thin – ranging from seven to 90 kilometres deep. Below the crust is a layer of very hot rock called the mantle. The upper part is almost solid. The lower part is more liquid. Below that is the outer **core** of liquid metal. The inner core is a ball of metal hotter than the surface of the Sun.

Faults

Deep cracks called **faults** lie on the borders where plates meet. Most earthquakes strike along these fault lines. **Volcanoes erupt** here too.

Shifting Plates

Earth's **tectonic plates** are not fixed in one place. They drift very slowly over the face of the Earth. The plates are probably set in motion by swirling currents in the semi-liquid rock below.

▼ Two hundred million years ago, all land on Earth was clustered into a single continent.

Continental drift

Over millions of years, drifting plates carry the continents across the globe. This movement is called **continental drift**.

Most tectonic plates shift just two to three centimetres per year. That's about as fast as your fingernails grow. Some move more quickly, at up to 15 centimetres a year.

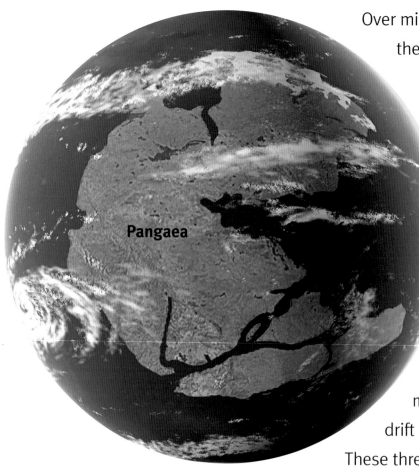

Pangaea

Types of fault

As plates drift across the globe, they may slowly crash together. Or they may drift apart, or scrape past one another. These three different movements create three types of **fault**.

Push, pull and shove

Where two plates collide on land, the ground between crumples upwards to form a range of mountains, such as the Himalayas. Where plates pull apart, a deep gap called a **rift valley** forms. Red-hot rock wells up to fill the gap. This creates a **volcano**. Earthquakes strike where plates scrape past one another.

◀ Volcanoes erupt where plates pull apart. This volcano is on Iceland, in the centre of the Atlantic Ocean. This ocean is slowly getting wider, as plates drift apart.

 SUPERCONTINENT

Around 250 million years ago, all land masses on Earth were joined together. This made one vast continent, which we call Pangaea. As plates drifted, the supercontinent split up. The pieces drifted very slowly across the oceans. Eventually they reached their present positions – but continental drift continues today.

Where
Earthquakes Strike

Almost all earthquakes strike at **faults**, because Earth's **crust** is weakest here. These lines of weakness are dangerous places to live.

Ring of fire

The Pacific Ocean lies on top of one large plate. The rim of the plate runs right around the ocean's edges. Earthquakes are common along this long fault. Fiery **volcanoes** also **erupt** here. For this reason, the rim of the Pacific is called the Ring of Fire.

▼ **This diagram shows the three different types of fault. Yellow arrows show which way the crust is moving.**

Down below the sea

As the sea floor spreads, plates near the edges of the ocean crash into other plates that carry land. When this happens, the ocean plate dives down below the other plate. Deep underground, the ocean crust melts. Then red-hot rock surges upwards. **Lava** bursts through to form a line of volcanoes on land.

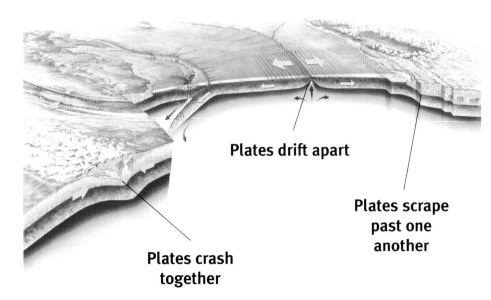

Plates drift apart

Plates scrape past one another

Plates crash together

Danger on land

Earthquakes also strike along fault lines that are mostly on land. They are quite common along a fault that runs east from near Italy to Turkey, India and Russia. Unfortunately, cities grew up here long before people understood what caused earthquakes.

▲ **This building in Kobe collapsed in the 1995 quake.**

CASE STUDY

Kobe, 1995

Japan is located where three **tectonic plates** meet. This is why earthquakes are common there. In 1995 an earthquake hit the port of Kobe in southern Japan. Many buildings collapsed and fires broke out. Much of the city burned and more than 5,000 people died.

What Happens in an **Earthquake?**

Tension builds up underground as plates push, pull or scrape past each other. When the tension gets too great, the rocks shatter. Slabs of rock jolt into new positions. The jolt causes a quake.

▼ **Shock waves ripple outwards from the focus of an earthquake.**

Deep below

Most earthquakes happen deep underground. The centre of the quake is called the **focus**. The effect is usually worst on the surface directly above. This point is called the **epicentre**.

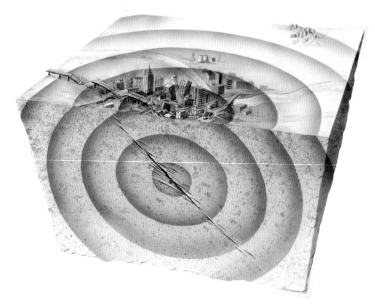

Minor quakes called **foreshocks** may hit before the main earthquake. **Aftershocks** shake the ground for days or weeks afterwards as rocks settle down.

Shock waves

Ripples of energy spread out from the focus in all directions. These are called **seismic waves** or shock waves. The ground can heave up and down like a ship in a storm.

Wave after wave

Earthquakes produce two main types of seismic waves. **Body waves** travel through the Earth. **Surface waves** spread across the surface. Some waves move up and down. Others travel from side to side. The most damaging waves move in both directions.

◀ This highway collapsed during the Kobe quake.

CASE STUDY

Antioch, 526 CE

The first recorded earthquake struck in what is now Turkey in 526 CE. It rocked the city of Antioch, where people had gathered for a religious festival. Homes and temples collapsed, oil lamps fell over and fires started. Around 250,000 people may have died. Further shocks hit the area in 528 and 588 CE.

Undersea Quakes

Earthquakes often shake the ocean floor. This is because many fault lines lie underwater. The Atlantic and Indian Oceans both lie on top of major **faults**. So does the Mediterranean Sea.

Reaching land

If an undersea earthquake strikes, shock waves often reach the land. Earthquakes that rock the bed of the Mediterranean are regularly felt in Italy. In 1908 around 120,000 people died in Italy when a quake struck just offshore. **Seismic waves** from earthquakes travel far across the oceans.

▶ **Pictures taken from the air show the coast of Indonesia before and after the 2004 quake.**

Tsunamis

Undersea quakes sometimes cause giant waves called **tsunamis**. As the sea floor shakes, huge masses of water slosh up, down or sideways. Waves spread outwards in all directions like ripples from a stone tossed in a lake.

Out in the open ocean the waves are quite low. But they race across the sea at up to 800 kilometres per hour. They rear up as they reach shallow water. Then, waves up to 30 metres high smash onto the coast.

▲ Poseidon, Greek god of the oceans, was believed to cause earthquakes. The horse was his symbol. The legend of the wooden horse used to capture the city of Troy may refer to an earthquake.

 CASE STUDY

Indian Ocean, 2004

On 26 December 2004 a massive earthquake shook the bed of the Indian Ocean. The quake struck close to Indonesia in South-East Asia. The quake and giant waves wrecked the coast of Indonesia. Tsunamis spread across 4,500 kilometres of ocean. They smashed onto distant coasts. Altogether, 283,000 people died.

Watching for
Earthquakes

▼ An early seismograph from Italy.

The study of earthquakes is called **seismology**. Nowadays scientists understand the causes of earthquakes. They know where they are likely to strike and have ways of watching for them. However, earthquakes still strike without warning.

Measuring quakes

Seismographs are instruments that measure shaking. They can record both earthquakes and minor quakes, called **tremors**. In a basic seismograph, a pen held over a roll of paper draws a line. If the ground shakes, the line becomes jagged. In modern versions, the line appears on a computer screen instead.

A single seismograph cannot show exactly where an earthquake struck. Readings from three machines in different places are used to pinpoint the **epicentre** of the quake.

New techniques

Satellites circling the Earth measure shifts in rocks far below. At ground level, lasers and other instruments measure tiny rock movements. These instruments are often positioned along **faults**. If rocks start to bulge, it can be a warning that an earthquake is about to strike.

▲ Japanese children practise what to do if an earthquake strikes.

ANIMALS AND EARTHQUAKES

Animals seem able to sense natural changes that occur just before an earthquake. Dogs are known to howl. Cocks start crowing. In Thailand, elephants fled inland before the **tsunami** struck in 2004. In 1975, experts in the Chinese city of Haicheng noticed animals behaving strangely. Everyone left the city. A few hours later, an earthquake struck.

Living through an
Earthquake

An earthquake is terrifying for anyone caught up in it.
The shaking lasts only a few seconds, but whole towns
can be reduced to rubble.

During a quake

Before a major quake, **foreshocks** sometimes make windows rattle.
When the main quake strikes, the ground heaves. Glass shatters.
Buildings sway and topple. Bridges and railway tracks twist and break.

In the country

In open country, earthquakes
are less dangerous for people.
In 1811–1812, a series of major
quakes hit New Madrid in
southern USA. The land sank
and whole new lakes formed.
However, not many people
lived in the region, so there
were relatively few deaths.

▶ **These houses collapsed
when a quake hit San
Francisco, USA, in 1989.**

Earthquake scales

Scientists have invented several scales to measure earthquakes. The Richter scale measures the amount of shaking on a scale of 1 to 10. Quakes that rate less than 3 cannot be felt. Severe quakes measure 7 to 8. The most violent rate over 9.

The Modified Mercalli scale rates the damage quakes cause as a way of comparing them. A scale of Roman numbers is used: I to XII. Quakes rated I are very slight. Scale VII quakes shake bricks loose. Scale XII quakes cause total destruction.

CASE STUDY

Tangshan, 1976

In 1976 an earthquake shook the Chinese city of Tangshan. It measured 7.8 on the Richter scale. The quake destroyed most of the city. More than 500,000 people died. Buildings had not been stoutly built, because earthquakes had not struck the region before.

▲ In 1970 an earthquake in Peru started a **landslide** in the mountains. The town of Yungay was buried. Only this statue was left standing.

Disaster!

The shaking of an earthquake lasts only seconds, but the danger lasts for much longer. **Aftershocks** often follow the main quake.

Dangerous cities

Many people die if an earthquake strikes a city. People may be hit by falling **debris**, or they can get trapped by falling buildings. Others die if roads, bridges and underground railways collapse.

▼ **This train was wrecked when the earthquake hit Kobe, Japan, in 1995.**

In modern cities people can be showered by glass from tall buildings. In older districts flimsy buildings are flattened. Many people die in crowded slums where homes are not well built.

Aftershocks

Aftershocks can topple buildings damaged by the main quake. These minor quakes can strike days or even months afterwards. Aftershocks menace people trapped in buildings and also rescue teams who arrive to help.

More danger

Earthquakes can also trigger further disasters. Fire can easily break out if gas and electricity lines are damaged. **Landslides** and **avalanches** may strike in steep or snowy areas. Floods can result if the quake weakens a dam or wall built to hold back a river or the sea.

▲ San Francisco lies in ruins after the earthquake and fire of 1906.

CASE STUDY

San Francisco, 1906

The city of San Francisco in California lies on a dangerous **fault**. It runs down the west coast of the USA and is called the San Andreas fault. In 1906 a huge earthquake rocked San Francisco. Fires then swept the city. About 2,800 people died in the quake and the fire.

After the **Quake**

The after-effects of an earthquake can last for many years. For people who have lost their homes and friends or family, life will never be the same.

Instant destruction

Major earthquakes cause complete chaos. Shattered buildings litter the streets. Many people are dead or dying. Survivors are often without shelter or outdoor clothing. There may be a shortage of food.

▼ **A rescue worker helps a boy to safety after an earthquake struck Colombia, South America, in 1999.**

Health problems

Emergency camps are set up to shelter survivors. Injured people need medical help, but it is often difficult for doctors and nurses to reach them. Wounds that aren't treated quickly can get worse.

Water supplies are often polluted by **debris** or spilled chemicals, so clean water may be scarce. Bodies may be left unburied. Disease spreads quickly in these conditions.

Shattered lives

After a major earthquake, nothing is working normally. Hospitals, shops, schools and work places are all closed. People have lost loved ones. Survivors are dazed and grieving. Everyone struggles to come to terms with the disaster that has occurred.

◀ People pray on the site of a ruined mosque following the Pakistan quake of 2005.

CASE STUDY

Pakistan and Kashmir, 2005

In October 2005 a major quake hit Pakistan and Kashmir in the Himalayas. Towns and villages were destroyed. The capital of Pakistan was also damaged. Around 82,000 people died, and 3.3 million were left homeless.
Landslides blocked roads so help could not get through. Many survivors had little shelter during the harsh winter that followed.

To the **Rescue**

After a major quake, emergency teams hurry to the disaster area. Local, national and often international teams work together to save lives.

▼ Survivors lived in tents for months following the Pakistan quake of 2005.

Cut off

Just reaching the stricken area may be very difficult. Roads may be blocked. Railways and bridges may be down. Telephone and electricity lines may be damaged. Often, the only way to reach the disaster zone is by helicopter. Supplies are sometimes dropped by plane.

First tasks

When rescue workers arrive, their first job is to search for people in the wreckage. This work is often done with the help of dogs or robots, because it can be very dangerous. Injured people are treated by doctors. All survivors are given food, water and clothing.

Living in camps

Survivors are often asked to leave the disaster zone. This is called **evacuation**. Emergency camps are set up. Aid organizations and charities work to raise money for local people who have lost everything.

▲ This robot searches for survivors in buildings wrecked by earthquakes.

TRAPPED IN THE WRECKAGE

After an earthquake hits a city, people are often trapped in the wreckage. Rescue workers have to proceed carefully because dangerous rubble could shift again. Specially trained dogs are used to sniff out survivors. Heat-sensing equipment can help to find people hidden under rubble. Robots are used in places that are too dangerous for people to go.

Rebuilding

▼ **This building in San Francisco has been built to survive an earthquake.**

The damage done by earthquakes can take years to repair. Survivors return when it is safe. People start to rebuild their homes and pick up their lives.

A new start

Before rebuilding can start, **debris** from the earthquake must be cleared away. Dangerous buildings are pulled down. Homes are rebuilt. Schools, shops, hospitals, factories and offices open, and life begins again.

Going home

Survivors often wish to return to live in the area they know, even if there is risk of future earthquakes. In any case, the area at risk can be huge. There may be nowhere else for people to go.

Homes can be built more strongly than before. But this can be expensive. In poor countries, people may not be able to afford to build houses that are more secure.

Quake-proof building

Buildings can be designed to stand up to minor earthquakes. Tall buildings can be built with a flexible framework. This allows them to move and sway, rather than shatter in an earthquake. Some buildings have shock absorbers built into their foundations.

▲ A survivor looks at damage caused by the Armenian earthquake of 1988.

CASE STUDY

Spitak, Armenia, 1988

In 1988, a powerful earthquake wrecked the town of Spitak in Armenia, western Asia. Apartment blocks, schools and hospitals had been cheaply built. They collapsed in ruins. International experts gave advice on rebuilding work, but local people couldn't afford to make all the changes they advised.

Future Quakes

Areas along **fault** lines are always at risk of earthquakes. Cities such as San Francisco in the USA and Kobe in Japan are always in some danger. But no one can be sure exactly when or where the next big quake will strike.

▼ The San Andreas fault in California can be seen clearly from the air.

Sliding or sticking?

Some fault lines are more active than others. Along some faults, rocks slide easily. Small quakes are common, but big ones are rare. In other areas, the rocks get stuck and the tension builds up. Eventually a major earthquake strikes.

Studying records

Scientists study the history of earthquakes in a region. These records can help to predict when the next one is due. Experts believe that San Francisco may be hit by a serious quake within the next 20 years.

This table shows how often major and minor earthquakes strike. Serious quakes are far less common than tiny ones.

RICHTER-SCALE RATING	HOW OFTEN?
0.5–2.0	8,000 per day
5	800 per year
7	18 per year
9	1 in 20 years

Getting ready

Earthquake drills take place in cities that are prone to earthquakes. People practise what to do in an emergency. If experts believe a serious quake is about to strike, they can order an **evacuation**. However, earthquakes still strike out of the blue, causing chaos.

▲ Naples in southern Italy lies in an earthquake zone.

MASSIVE POWER

Earthquakes are incredibly powerful natural forces. That is one reason why we will never be able to control them. The biggest quakes release the explosive power of about a thousand nuclear bombs.

TEN OF THE DEADLIEST EARTHQUAKES

When	Where	Casualties
1556	Shaanxi, China	830,000
1976	Tangshan, China	255,000–655,000
2004	Indian Ocean	283,000
1138	Aleppo, Syria	230,000
1920	Gansu, China	200,000
1927	Qinghai, China	200,000
856	Damghan, Iran	200,000
893	Ardabil, Iran	150,000
1923	Kanto region, Japan	143,000
1948	Ashgabat, Turkmenistan	110,000

FURTHER INFORMATION

Books

Explore It: Earthquakes and Volcanoes by Anne Rooney (Silver Dolphin, 2006)
Eyewitness: Volcanoes and Earthquakes by Susanna Van Rose (Dorling Kindersley, 2004)
Horrible Geography: Earth-Shattering Earthquakes by Anita Ganeri (Scholastic, 2000)
Turbulent Planet: Shaky Ground: Earthquakes by Mary Colson (Raintree, 2005)

Websites

news.bbc.co.uk/1/hi/world/4126809.stm
A quick guide to tectonics and the causes of earthquakes.

science.howstuffworks.com/earthquake.htm
A more detailed guide to how earthquakes happen.

www.exploratorium.edu/faultline/index.html
Some activities that help you find out about how earthquakes work.

DVDs

The American Experience: The Great San Francisco Earthquake (1988; DVD: 2006)
Earthquake directed by Mark Robson (1974; DVD: 2005)
Earthquake: Nature Unleashed directed by Tibor Takacs (2005)
National Geographic: Forces of Nature directed by George Casey (1999; DVD: 2004)

GLOSSARY

aftershock
When the ground shakes as it settles down after an earthquake.

avalanche
When a large mass of snow slides downhill.

body wave
A seismic wave that travels through the Earth.

continental drift
The extremely slow movement of the continents across the surface of the Earth.

core
The centre of the Earth where the rocks are incredibly hot.

crust
The hard, rocky outer surface of the Earth.

debris
Broken pieces of rock, brick work or other material.

epicentre
The place on the Earth's surface directly above the point where an earthquake strikes.

erupt
When a volcano comes to life and gives off lava, gas and steam.

evacuation
When people are ordered to leave an area because of danger.

fault
A deep crack that marks a boundary between tectonic plates. Faults are also called fault lines.

focus
The point underground where rocks shatter during an earthquake.

foreshock
A minor earthquake that shakes the ground before the main quake strikes.

landslide
When a mass of soil and rock slips downhill.

lava
Red-hot rock that surges up from deep underground and erupts from a volcano.

mantle
The deep layer of red-hot, semi-liquid rocks beneath the crust.

rift valley
A deep valley that forms either on land or undersea, where tectonic plates are drifting apart.

seismic wave
Also called a shock wave. A wave of energy released by an earthquake.

seismograph
An instrument for measuring the shaking caused by earthquakes.

seismology
The scientific study of earthquakes.

surface wave
A seismic wave that travels across the Earth's surface.

tectonic plate
One of the giant rocky sections that make up the Earth's outer crust. These sections are constantly moving, floating on the mantle below.

tremor
The shaking caused by a minor earthquake.

tsunami
A massive wave caused by an earthquake, landslide or volcanic eruption on the seabed.

volcano
A weak point in the Earth's crust through which lava, steam and gas escape during an eruption.

INDEX

Page numbers in **bold** refer to illustrations.